"... down to the sea again..."* again and again

John B. Moullette, Ed. D.
Able-Seaman-Quartermaster
Certificate of Identification
Z853680

*With apologies to John Masefield (1878-1967),
British poet laureate (1930-1967):
"I must down to the sea again
To the lonely sea and sky, and
all I ask is a tall ship and
a star to stear [sic] her by."

Private Printing, September 2010

© 2010, 2013 John B. Moullette

All rights reserved.

John Brinkley Moullette
3937 Winding Road
Fort Garland, Colorado 81133

ISBN: 1484944259
ISBN-13: 978-1484944257

DEDICATION

To Those Who Go Down to the Sea in Ships.

"Ships (and guns) are called 'she' because wars are fought by lonely men." – Unknown

CONTENTS

	Acknowledgments	i
	down to the sea again, again and again	1
1	An Awareness and a Yearning	2
2	First Ship Preparation	7
3	Pick-up Job Training	9
4	The Drill	12
5	Preparing for Life at Sea	15
	On Job Training	19
6	Climbing Jacob's Ladder	20
7	Duties of A Seaman	22
8	Addendum	27
	Incidents at Sea	28
	Afterthoughts	38
9	Post World War II	40
10	Naval Institute and Other Certificates	43
11	Scuba Diving	44
	Ancillaries	46
	Appendices	54

ACKNOWLEDGMENTS

Primarily this is an accounting – not a novel and not a novella – of one part of my life before I ever earned a diploma or a degree. Hopefully, if my kids read it, my children will see me differently than they saw me when I was raising a family. Within, there might be "some answers" and a different picture of Dad. The account is from memory, but for assistance, I wish to thank those institutions and persons who were helpful. They are:

>National Archives and Records Administration
>Old Military and Civilian Records
>Textual Archives Service Division
>Susan Abbott
>700 Pennsylvania Avenue, NW
>Washington, DC 20408-0001

>United States Coast Guard
>National Vessel Documentation Center
>Jennifer R. Barney
>Records and Research Assistant
>792 T.J Jackson Drive
>Falling Waters, WV 25419-9052

And to:
>F.O. "Clarke" Valles
>Apt. 108
>7865 East Mississippi Avenue
>Denver, CO 80247

for providing me with World War II era information about

the:
> U.S. Maritime Service Training Station
> Sheepshead Bay, New York

and for inviting me to join merchant mariner veterans in Denver, Colorado. I regret I didn't take him up on his offer.

With the deepest appreciation to my good friend Leland Dirks for his steadfast efforts at editing, formatting, and publishing. Without his gentlemanly urging this 'ship would never have reached port let alone left the dock.'

Down to the Sea Again, Again and Again

1 AN AWARENESS AND A YEARNING

If, as a young boy, you had lived on the shores of the Delaware River, which flows between Philadelphia and Camden, New Jersey, prior to World War II you would have had an awareness of ships, boats and barges – more so than an awareness of recreational, water borne vessels beyond the hand-rowed dinghy, the canoe, kayak, or the single-masted, hollow structured sail boat powered by the wind.

Both sides of the river harbored docks, warehouses, ships and shipyards for the docking and repairing of freighters – domestic and foreign – that delivered and transported goods and materials domestically and internationally.

Occasionally an oil tanker could be observed going up or down the river – to or from – an oil terminal on Petty Island off the center of the channel above the Delaware River Bridge, now the Benjamin Franklin. Two major shipyards were situated – one each – on both sides: the Philadelphia Navy Yard and the New York Shipyard in Camden. Minor yards such as Cramp's were on the Pennsy side and Mathys on the Jersey side. Any beach walker on the Jersey bank could observe these ships; and, with an imaginative mind a young boy could fantasize that one day he would sail in such a ship. I did!

Quitting school during the war by "dropping-out" of Woodrow Wilson High School in Camden, I worked at the Mathys Shipyard where I observed the building of ships from the keel-up to launching and once stood on the bow of a freighter – holding fast to the flag staff – as it was christened and slid down the railway to its natural environment for its trial run and eventual sailing to foreign lands to deliver supplies to America's fighting men and women around the world. What an experience that was to watch a beautiful, young lady swing the christening bottle of Champagne against the hull and – as the ship descended – feel the river current grasp the ship and send it on its way for "fitting out." I wondered: "would I ever have the opportunity to sail in such a ship?" Yes, I would!

World War II presented me with a dilemma: join the Marines as my father had in World War One or go to sea with the American merchant marine? I chose the former and – as such – I eventually sailed in troopships, landing ships (LSTs), Higgins boats, and amphibious tractors (Amtracs). A boyhood dream to be a Marine had been realized but these shipboard experiences were as a trooper headed in harm's way and not as a working seaman beyond: "sweepers, man your brooms for a clean sweep-down fore and aft."

The war ended in the Pacific and I returned from China in the standard way for that era: by troopship.

Again I was faced with another dilemma at the age of 19 "going on" 20: what does a young man with three years of Marine Corps service – some of it in combat – do for the immediate future?

I tried returning to high school at Temple University in Philadelphia but after a few weeks I decided that schooling at this particular time of my life was not for me. So, "dropping-out" again and walking south on Philadelphia's Broad Street, I spied a very large banner that read: "America Needs a Strong Merchant Marine." There was the answer: "go to sea" – another boyhood dream!

But, how to find a ship? Being on North Broad Street, I realized the waterfront was just about 14 blocks away to the east. There – and right then – I decided I would start my quest just north of the Delaware River Bridge. I immediately walked to the waterfront – opposite the New Jersey shoreline – which started south of Cramp's Shipyard. For the next three days I covered the waterfront and boarded ships either by a gangplank or by an accommodation ladder. At the top of each I would be confronted by a watch stander who wanted to know my business and I would ask: "Is there a berth for a seaman aboard this ship?" North or south of the bridge the answer was always the same: "No"! If you want a berth you must go through the Union Hall," which I learned would be one of three: the Seaman's Union of the Pacific (SUP), the Seaman's International Union (SIU), or the National Maritime Union (NMU).

What to do? Looking in a phone book I found there was an NMU Hall in the vicinity. I took off for there and when I found it, I walked into a crowded, smoke filled room of unemployed merchant sailors all waiting to be called to fill a berth, on any ship, bound anywhere, as a messman, a deck worker, or in the "black gang" – not a racial slur. When I got to the front of the line I stated my purpose to the agent. After a few questions he told me: "There are no berths for non-ticketed persons and who do not belong to the Union." He continued: "Your chances of finding a berth and getting ticketed are slim to nil as all the men in this Hall and around the country are "veterans" of numerous ship convoys who sailed the oceans in harm's way. Good-luck, next!" So, being a Marine Corps veteran of the Pacific and China held no sway in this situation. Having lost a family friend at sea – Harry J. Mote, Jr., second engineer aboard the SS *Meriwether Lewis*, March 2, 1943 in the Atlantic Ocean – I could well understand the policy and the feelings of the men in the NMU hall at this time.

So, what to do and where to go?

Ah! The Custom House at Second and Chestnut Streets in Philadelphia where I had enlisted in the Marines in the late fall of 1943 – just after the battle for the island of Tarawa in the South Pacific!

At the Custom House and in the duty room of the Coast Guard I met a young petty officer who informed me that in order to get "ticketed" one had to get a "letter of promised employment" from a shipping company or agent. He knew of one: the Atlantic Refining Company (ARCO) at 28th and Passyunk Avenue on the Schuykill River. Off I went by trolley car – south on Broad and west on Passyunk.

In the marine employment office of the ARCO refining plant I was met by a distinguished gentleman who had, obviously, been a naval officer in the recent war. He was attired in a black and white checkered sport jacket with gray trousers and "spit shined," black shoes. He asked me my business and when I told him, he said: "we are hiring but only veterans of the recent war." And, I said; "Well, I am a veteran!" His response: "You are?" He wanted to know more and I gave him the details. His instructions were to return with papers – an honorable discharge, a birth certificate, a social security card, and a draft card. Enlisting in the Marines at 17, I didn't have the latter but procured one from the Draft Board in Camden which classified me as 4-C returning veteran subject to recall in the event of a national emergency. That's another story!

Within a week I returned to ARCO and presented Mr. Charles Waters with the documents and he immediately issued me a "letter of promised employment" which I presented to the petty officer at the Custom House. Without hesitation, I was issued a US Mariner Document in the form of a laminated card (Z853680) certifying me to sail as a wiper (engine room), ordinary seaman, or messman. In the winter of 1946 I sailed out of Portsmouth, Rhode Island as a wiper aboard the Steam Ship *Atlantic States* bound for Port Arthur, Texas and the ARCO refinery and terminal on the Sabine River.

2 FIRST SHIP PREPARATION

Prior to joining the *Atlantic States* I was not unfamiliar with the maritime service or seamanship. At the age of 11 I attended meetings (too young to join) of the Sea Scouts – a division of the Boy Scouts in Cramer Hill, a suburb of Camden. There I learned some basics: how to tie – beyond a shoe string knot and a granny – a square knot, a clove hitch and a two half hitch as well as shipboard nomenclature – bow, stern, port (left) and starboard. In the summers I was the guest of a family friend – Gus Mote brother of Harry – at the Mote family seashore resort at Barnegat Beach. Here, "Uncle Gus" introduced me to the Sunfish sailboat and taught me how to set the rudder, step the mast, hoist the single sail, and sail with the wind in Barnegat Bay.

When the war came – I was 14 (going on 15) and I joined the Camden unit of the American Coast Patrol (ACP) – the role of which was to support the New Jersey state militia in the protection of highway bridges, electrical installations, and water towers from saboteurs who might land on the Jersey coast, which they did but not on "my watch" or on any Jersey coast. During this tour I learned basic formations, drills and military courtesy: "Yes sir," "No sir," and, "By your leave, sir" as well as basic methods of patrolling and watch standing.

At the age of 16, I left high school and went to work – full-time – at the Mathys Shipyard; first as a cleaner and later as an Ozalid Operator in the drafting department. At the latter job I was responsible for reproducing white prints from drawings and for delivering same to lofts and shipboard compartments. This job allowed me to wander the yard and find my way around ships by way of ladders, alley ways, decks, holds, engine rooms, cabins, lockers and lazerettes as well as to climb masts – fore and aft – and to observe the workers: riggers, iron workers, welders and burners, electricians, carpenters and ship fitters.

In the Marine Corps – at the age of 17 – I sailed across the Pacific bound for a war zone and into the Yellow Sea aboard a troopship which was a converted from a freighter to an APA-attack personnel auxiliary. On board we roomed in a hold, shacked up in a bunk, showered in a head and stood watches with the sailors (swabbies) fore and aft and along the railings. This experience brought me face to face with the elements: storms, heavy seas, cold weather, and seasickness. With a full marching pack and rifle we Marines disembarked – four abreast – by way of a cargo net into landing boats for the trip ashore and into harm's way.

3 PICK-UP JOB TRAINING

Prior to sailing as a wiper in the *Atlantic States* – Captain H.M. Lauritzen, Commanding – my experience with tools was limited: hammer, nails and saws to build bunk houses, improvised mallets to pound tent stakes, screwdrivers, wrenches, and hand pumps to repair flat tires on my bike. In the Marine Corps the only implement required was a "combination tool" seated in the buttplate behind a hinged trap door in the stock of the rifle. This tool consisted of a bullet size implement for a cleaning patch to clean the receiver and an attached screwdriver to remove the muzzle plug to get at the gas cylinder in the M-1 Garand 30.06 rifle.

   So, being a wiper, below decks, and in the engine room was a new experience and an introduction to new tools. Work consisted of cleaning up after the fireman, the water tender, the oiler and assisting (gofer) the pump man, the machinist, and the engineer. Beyond "soogieing," wiping-up oil and grease, chipping and painting there were "lines" to be traced: water, oil and steam "for leaks. When found, these required the removal of valves, gaskets, couplers and the replacing of same. Open end, box and monkey wrenches (sometimes with a cheater) were required. Often times a block and tackle was needed or a "come-along." This could take place anywhere: on deck, in the shaft alley, and any place 'tween deck spaces in the engine room. Work below was always hot and dirty.

My first voyage was a unique experience: I was paid $105.00 per month, stood one, single watch of eight hours per day (weekends free), ate three meals a day and a "night lunch," and was berthed in a three man forecastle (foc'sle) with an ensuite hot water sink and mirror, a single desk with chair, and a personal locker adjoining the tier bunks. What a difference from the Marine Corps and troopships where I was paid $60.00 per month, was expected to stand watches of any length – time off was subject to demands – and chow consisting, often, of K or C rations.

But, something was missing – working in the open, watching the sea go by, and observing the ship's heading, as well as the variations in the weather. I began to understand me and my lack of aptitude for mechanics and a desire – and ability – to be a marine engineer.

My first voyage lasted 38 days and when the opportunity was presented I transferred to the deck gang as an ordinary seaman, day worker. This transfer was facilitated by the Chief Mate and bos'n (boatswain) and no doubt encouraged by the First Engineer. I remained aboard the SS *Atlantic States* and signed new articles to sail as a "deck hand."

My first tour in the *Atlantic States* allowed me to observe the work of the deck department and deck hands – day workers and watch standers. Before sailing and on the advice of an old sailor I went to the Philadelphia waterfront and found a "ships' chandler" where I outfitted myself with work clothes for warm and cold weather as well as clothes for inclement weather. The latter was a three piece, water resistant, set of oilskins, which consisted of: bib type pants, a slouch hat with a wide flexible brim, and an over the hip jacket. Before leaving the ship a "salty-old Norwegian" sailor advised me to pick-up a sheathed knife with a good blade edge and a "fold in" marlinespike as well as a pocket whetstone; and, while I was at it to get a few three sided stitch needles and a palm to sew canvas. I picked up three of the latter of different sizes and strengths. Outfitted with new outerwear that included ankle high, cord shoes – oil resistant and non-slip, I returned to the ship for the next OJT experience as an ordinary seaman.

The next day – February 4, 1947 – the SS *Atlantic States* – Captain Werner Appleton – Commanding, sailed.

4 THE DRILL

Prior to sailing, the 13 members of the deck gang consisting of six (6) able-seaman, three (3) watch-standing ordinaries, and three (3) day workers (ordinaries) and one (1) bos'n assembled aft of the shelter deck and were assigned stations and duties by the bos'n – the leader of the gang – for getting the ship cleared of its moorings and getting underway.

The watch standers came from the three – around the clock – watches: morning, forenoon, and afternoon (0400-0800, 0800-1200, 1200-1600 repeated later as 1600-2000, 2000-2400, and 0100-0400).

The twelve were assigned by the bos'n as follows: one "on-duty" able-seaman to the wheel house to man the helm and one to the bow with the ordinary seaman; two (2) able – seaman and a watch ordinary to the fan-tail on the stern; and two able-seamen and an ordinary midships on the main deck. The three day workers – all ordinaries – were assigned as follows: one forward, one aft to the stern, and one midships along the railing.

The deck gang – as required – handled all lines (fore, aft and midships) to release the ship from its moorings. Those deck hands forward had the added responsibility of hauling in and setting the anchor and hosing it down as it passed thru the hawse pipe and dropped into the chain locker below deck and saw to it the anchor was seated against the ship's hull.

Once the order was given to "lower the ball and heave her (the anchor) in" the work began to get underway. The bos'n manned the steam winch to haul in the anchor and the chief mate watched the anchor's progress out of the water, up along the hull and seated with the flukes facing outward.

Bow lines would be shipped first, stern lines next to allow the ship's bow to swing away from the dock – and simultaneously – the spring lines midship for the ship's final release from the dock. Once the ship was underway on duty watch standers moved to the bridge, off duty watch standers and day workers set about stowing lines: bow lines in a forward "hold," stern lines aft in a "lazerette," and spring lines flaked in the "shelter deck" midships.

After a short coffee break, the deck gang went to work securing the ship for sea and for crossing the sand bar into the open ocean. Entry way hatches and tank tops were closed, dogged down and made watertight. All loose gear was stowed or made fast. Heaving lines, blocks and tackle and ladders – such as a Jacob were stored in the shelter deck with hand tools in respected places – a place for everything and everything in its place.

A ship is not indigenous to the sea. Fresh and salt water play havoc with a ship in the forms of rust, corrosion, and rot – rust on iron and steel, corrosion on copper and brass, and rot on wood, hemp and canvas. Once the ship is underway maintenance begins: chipping, scraping, wire brushing and painting on metal, greasing on brass plates and metal work on machinery, and marlinespike seamanship on canvas and hemp lines – 3/16" to 4".

5 PREPARING FOR LIFE AT SEA

In post World War II in American merchant fleets there was no formal training programs as you might have found in industry, manufacturing or construction. Any merchant sailors – during the war – who had wanted to "go to sea" may have gotten their training in a government operated training facility – on the east coast – at Sheepshead Bay, Brooklyn, NY, under the guidance of the United States Maritime Commission and the United States Coast Guard. When the war ended that training ended, as there was no further need for "convoy sailors."

When I sailed – late 1946 – the mode of training was "pick-up" – one learns while one earns; and, therefore there were no training categories such as: apprentice, journeyman, and master journeyman that led to one becoming an artisan with the appropriate certification as an artificer. Signing on as an ordinary seaman I quickly learned that the nature of the work aboard ship required one to be enthusiastic, intuitive and eager to tackle any job assigned with the intention of mastering the tasks and jobs. Slackers were not welcomed! And, the "teachers" were "ancient mariners" who learned their skills on the old sailing ships, coal fired steamships and they "came up" through the "hawse pipe."

The major-domo on deck was the boatswain (bos'n) who assigned tasks and work and who followed-up on the assignments and the men responsible. A good bos'n (and I served under several) would take a "new hand" and show him around the ship before sailing and mate the novice with an experienced hand.

The day's work began at 0800 – after a hearty breakfast – for non-watch standers and concluded at 1700 hours with intermittent breaks for lunch and coffee. In my case the bos'n took me forward to the bos'n's locker, the paint locker, the tool crib, the chain locker in the fore castle and then mid-ships to the rigging room and pointed out hemp and cord, canvas, blocks and tackles, stoppers, heaving lines and associated hand tools. Along the way he pointed out the steam and electric winches and capstans. Anything else I was to learn on the go. But, he did point out that an oil tanker had twenty-seven – nine rows of three across – cavernous, cargo holds to contain jet fuel, aviation gas, furnace oil, petrol and crude oil. These, he noted, needed butterworthing (cleaning) periodically as did the holds for "bunker fuel" that fired-up the boilers.

The major and daily tasks of the seaman were to maintain the ship above the main deck – fore and aft of topside housing – and, at times, over the side of the ship as well as masts and kingposts.

Getting underway from the dock, the seamen are tasked to raise the anchor, ship the lines, and stow all running gear for a safe voyage to the next port of call.

On deck a seaman is never without a knife and stone to sharpen the knife, a marlinespike, a pocket crescent wrench, and a sheathed ¾" open wrench with a pointed end to tighten down nuts and bolts and to hold flanges in place. A "cheater" to apply leverage to the wrench needs to be accessible.

In inclement weather – beyond a peripheral inspection of the ship – all work is done in the shelter deck: oiling and greasing tools and friction equipment, repairing hemp and cord, sewing canvas, splicing, whipping, and chaffing.

Aboard ship there is always work to be done – corrosion in the tanks can eat a ship up in 20+ years and rust and decay can inhibit the life of a ship.

Fore and aft the new ordinary seaman learns there are permanently installed bollards or bits where round turns of heavy hemp line hold the ship to the dock. Getting underway requires theses lines to be shipped and hauled in by "Norwegian steam" at first then by the steam winch or electric capstan to bring them on deck where they are flaked out and made fast prior to stowing. If the ships is anchored the anchor – a Danforth – is hauled in first – upon command – by the steam winch since the anchor will weigh at least 5 tons and each link about 150 lbs. Most ships have 150 fathoms of chain (900') and 5-7 fathoms of chain are let out for each fathom of water 90' of water, 15 fathoms, 90' of chain. One learns fast how important the steam winch is in hauling in and stowing the anchor and therefore one becomes acquainted with the essentials – drum brake and clutch lever, and speed control. Usually, the bos'n handles the winch and occasionally will allow a seaman to "get the hang of it." Down below the chain is not allowed to pyramid so one or two seamen will be ordered below to guide the links to a horizontal lay in the anchor locker.

The deck – at the bow – of an oil tanker is a formidable minefield of equipment and machinery; a steam windlass, gypsy heads (winches), capstans and bits – the latter for "tying-up" the ship.

The major structure is the steam winch that holds the chain to the anchor. The chain is held in place by the windlass, which grasps each link and holds the anchor in place for dropping or bringing in the anchor. To use the gypsy heads to bring in the forward/bow lines the windlass must be disengaged by releasing the clutch and engaging the gypsy head winches.

Usually the anchor – if dropped – is hauled in first with the chain going immediately into the chain locker where the "bitter end" is firmly attached to the locker deck.

Once the anchor is set and made fast and the lines are secured, watches are manned and look outs posted on the bow and on the bridge as the ship gets underway – usually down a river where small boats and large ships are using the waterway – to assist in avoiding collisions.

ON JOB TRAINING

6 CLIMBING JACOB'S LADDER

On job training is the scheme for making headway as a seaman and for a career at sea. For about a year, the new seaman will work as a deck hand in order to become acquainted with life, work and duties aboard ship in any weather, at any time, and in all circumstances. As an experienced vocational educator it is easy to look back and identify the major training steps: apprentice, journeyman, and master. On deck, these would be recognized as: ordinary seaman, able seaman, and – quartermaster. With the appropriate officer recommendations where after 365 days at sea the seaman can "sit" for an exam by the United States Coast Guard in any major American port and upon passing that exam can be classified as an able seaman – 12 months. With this classification he can take on watch standing duties and continue to accept responsibilities for maintaining the ship, steering the ship, and loading and discharging the ship's cargo, and assisting in docking and "letting go" the ship.

Upon completing another 730 full days at sea the able seaman (AB) can take another Coast Guard exam – paper and "hands on" – and upon successful completion of these "milestones," the seaman is "ticketed" as an Able Seaman for life. This certification allows for the assumption of duties as a watch helmsman and/or as a bos'n. The former is responsible to the mate on duty.

In port or at sea duties and responsibilities are not inclusive to one job or task at a time; they are consolidated as required and performed as directed whether the seaman has one day at sea or the accumulated 1,095 required to become an Able Seaman for life.

The learning experiences and on-job training are truly "pick-up" throughout the first three years at sea and a young and inexperienced sailor needs to have a mentor. In my case my mentor was an "old salt" of Norwegian extraction by the name of Blackie who sailed in clipper ships, steam turbines, and diesel electric steel bottoms.

7 DUTIES OF A SEAMAN

To assist the interested and the motivated there are guidelines – to climb Jacob's ladder – by the Employment and Training Administration of the U. S. Department of Labor. These guidelines can be found in the DOL's Dictionary of Occupational Titles and enumerated in U. S. Coast Guard publications. During "the war," training was conducted at such institutions as the U. S. Merchant Marine Training Station at Sheepshead Bay, Brooklyn, NY. The training facility closed in 1947 and training was by on-job-training (OJT) after that for new, post war seaman such as I. However, at least one union picked up the responsibility after 1967 and that was the Seafarer's International Union (SIU) Harry Lunderberg School of Seamanship followed by the National Maritime Union's (NMU) Upgrading and Retraining School. Six state maritime academies provide training primarily at the baccalaureate level and graduate third officers for the deck and engine departments. The United States Military Sealift

Command (MSC) provides retraining for seaman primarily in fire prevention and suppression. Many two-year, community colleges provide education and training for the potential seafarer – based on local needs – and for those who wish to have a deepwater career.

I have attempted to identify the jobs and tasks of a seaman as I remember them from "pick-up" training aboard ship and at sea.

The DOT's job descriptions are specific but not all encompassing but they do provide a guide. They are herein enumerated.

<u>Ordinary Seaman</u>
911.687-030
Apprentice

The "Ordinary":
- stands deck department watches
- performs a variety of duties to preserve painted surfaces
- maintains lines, running gear and cargo-handling gear; keeps same in safe operating condition
- watches from bow of ship or wing of bridge for obstructions in path of ship
- turns wheel while observing compass to steer; and keeps ship on course
- mops (swabs) and washes down decks; uses hose to remove oil, dirt and debris
- chips and scrapes rust spots from deck, superstructure and sides of ship; uses hand or chipping hammer and wire brush
- paints chipped area; applies fish oil, undercoat and primer and finish
- splices wire rope; uses marlinespike, wire-cutters,

and twine
- splices hemp; uses marline-spike
- sews canvas; uses three sided needles as required

When the "ordinary" completes 365 days (8,760 hours minimum) at sea, the ordinary becomes eligible to "sit for" the Able Seaman ticket. With discharges signed by every Ships' Captain sailed under, the ordinary can present his documents to the nearest Coast Guard station/office and request to take the paper, oral and "hands on" tests for certification as an Able Seaman. Once certified as an Able Seaman the certificate is "good for life." This allows the AB to, eventually, serve as a quartermaster (helmsman) and boatswain (bos'n),

<u>Able Seaman (AB)</u>
911.364-010
Journeyman

The AB:
- performs tasks on board ship to watch for obstructions in vessel's path
- stands watch at bow and/or wing of bridge; and, "calls out" when ships or obstructions are seen
- maintains depth of water in shallow or unfamiliar waters; uses lead line; shouts information to bridge
- steers ship by wheel; uses emergency steering apparatus as directed by officer in charge (OIC) – a mate, captain or ship's pilot
- breaks out rigging and cargo handling gear; and maintains, overhauls and stows cargo handling gear
- maintains stationary rigging and running gear
- overhauls lifeboats and life boat equipment and gear

- operates lifeboat winches and falls

A major part of the AB test is the "hands on" handling of a lifeboat in the water. This generally is held "dock-side" with a 360° sweep in the boat to illustrate boat handling, stepping the mast, setting the rudder, and sailing "with the wind" to bring the lifeboat to dockside and disembarking passengers. When the AB is issued the Able Seaman ticket, the AB is considered by "all hands" to be a qualified "lifeboat man."

Monthly, aboard ship, fire, lifeboat and "man overboard" drills are held. At least once a year lifeboat handling water drills are held in ship anchored areas.

<u>AB-Quartermaster</u>
911.363.014
Master Craftsman

The AB-Quartermaster (helmsman):
- steers ship under the direction of the OIC or navigating officer
- maintains a designated compass course
- stands by wheel when ship is on "automatic pilot"
- verifies accuracy of course by comparing compass course with magnetic course
- relays specific signals to ships in vicinity by semaphore flags and signaling shutter light (blinker)
- directs maintenance crews in wheelhouse and quarter-deck maintenance when not "at the wheel"
- maintains ships log
- stands "gangway" watch in port; prevents unauthorized personnel from coming "on board"

At sea – usually the AB's second year at sea – the

quartermaster begins familiarization with dead reckoning, piloting, celestial and electronic navigation. The quartermaster maintains charts (maps at sea), and charting equipment such as: compass, dividers, parallel rulers, course recorders, pelorus and binnacles, log recording devices and rotators; begins to use a sextant (personal). And, the quartermaster maintains tide tables, tidal current tables, table distances between ports and sight reduction tables.

For the next two years – three total at sea – the quartermaster can, by practice and study, prepare for the license as a Third Mate or Officer of ocean going vessels. If successful the new licensee moves out of the foc'sle and into a cabin.

Often times an AB will choose to remain in the foc'sle and work as an AB-seaman and, when opportunity arises, sail as a boatswain.

Boatswain (Bos'n)
911.131-010

The AB-Bos'n:
- supervises able and ordinary seaman in their jobs and tasks on deck
- examines cargo handling gear and life-saving equipment
- supervises the repairing, maintenance or replacing of defective gear

The bos'n takes orders from the maintenance officer (usually a chief mate) and docking and departing instructions from the captain or the captain's surrogate – an officer.

8 ADDENDUM

When I went to sea – late 1940's-mid 1950's – there were no formal training programs where one learned to be a seaman.

After 30 + years as a vocational educator it is possible to equate seaman ratings (ordinary, able and quartermaster) to industry wide training programs of: apprentice, journeyman and master. In all cases certifications are required.

"Pick-up" training for a seaman was spotty and circumstantial. One observed, assumed responsibilities, did the jobs and the tasks, asked questions and – where and when available – obtained a handbook of sorts to help you know, understand and apply.

The ability to take the noted Dictionary of Occupational Titles (the DOT) and apply the jobs and tasks can be facilitated to "develop" a training program; one needs only to obtain a copy of:

- Moullette, Ed. D., John B. <u>Training Start-up and Planning Guide</u>. Tarpon Springs, FL, personal printing, 1989. 44 pp. illus. copyright number TXU-385-232 in the Library of Congress, Washington, D.C.

INCIDENTS AT SEA

After departing Camp Lejeune by troop train for travel west across the United States and after arriving at Union Station, Los Angeles, we Marines – in the hundreds – were shuttled by truck convoy south on US 101 to Navy Pier San Diego. There a navy band musically welcomed the Marines to board ship by an accommodation ladder. The ship was a converted freighter and an APA – Auxiliary Personnel Attack–troop transport bound for Northern China. On the tide – within minutes of our arrival – the ship "slipped its lines" and backed out to sea.

The first nautical words I heard that gave a definite command were: "lower the ball and heave her in!" Whenever a ship anchors – at sea, in an estuary, or in port – a black, lightweight ball is "run-up" the forward mast. This indicates to other ships the vessel is at anchor. When lowered it indicates the ship is "underway" – officially.

The sea trip – across the Pacific – lasted about four weeks before we arrived at Taku, China. In those weeks we Marines:

- stood "watches" around the clock and were alert for

other ships, submarine torpedoes and floating mines; and, of course, for anyone afloat from any other ship.
- grew accustomed to living in crowded quarters where our "bunks" – each one contained a Marine and his combat equipment.
- recognized BO and endured and showered and washed our clothes with seawater.
- waited in long lines to reach the "mess deck" and eat "chow," and to the "heads" or latrines.
- kept the living "quarters" clean and in "ship shape" condition by responding to the "boatswain's (bos'n's) whistle; "sweepers man your brooms for a clean sweep down fore and aft."
- stood "lookout watches" and with the "armed guards" in their gun turrets "manned" the 50 caliber machine guns and took target practice with same.
- experienced high seas, cold rain, and storms wearing minimum amount of weather gear while wearing a steel helmet.
- searched the ship for a "buddy" who apparently went "overboard" as a result of being sea sick – poor guy!
- crossed the 180th meridian – westbound – in latitude 40° 30' N and entered the Domain of the Golden Dragon – west of the International Date Line.
- passed thru the East China Sea and entered the Yellow Sea between China and the Korean Peninsula.
- off Taku, disembarked down a "cargo net" – (hands on the verticals; feet on the horizontals) – into a LCI – Landing Craft Infantry – for the trip ashore and

into "harm's way."

A year later the return to the States was in the troopship USS *John C. Breckenridge* – Buchanan's Vice-President; Jefferson Davis' Secretary of State and a CSA General. This was a shorter and speedier trip and was one of rest, relaxation and rehabilitation.

On both voyages – outbound-west and inbound-east – playing cards (gambling) was a part of "off-duty" life. Blackjack (21) was my favorite and I was relatively successful. Aboard the APA I was playing and winning so much so that a technical sergeant accused me of cheating and demanded a return of his losses. I refused!

He pulled me up off the "cargo hold," grabbed me by what Marines call "the stacking swivel" and slammed me up against the "bulkhead." Again, he demanded a return of his losses; again, I refused. Pulling his Kaybar knife from its scabbard, he pressed the point of the blade against my throat. Then, he backed down – which was a relief to me – and walked off without saying another word to me or the Marines watching on. Since he was a NCO and I a PFC I could have pressed charges – but didn't.

Returning in the troopship one year later to San Diego I won heavily and broke a buddy. Knowing his wife was meeting him "dockside," I returned 75% of his losses and he thanked me. And, there was still plenty of liberty money for a few drinks in a bar off Grant Square.

The Steam Ship *Atlantic States* was my first merchant ship in the American merchant marine or what the British call the merchant navy; and, it will always have a place in my memories. (see the Appendices and the Bibliography)

It was in the States where I learned more about me and my aptitudes or a lack of them; and, where I learned –

ultimately – to be a seaman and eventually a sailor. My first trip at sea was with the Atlantic Refining Company (ARCO) and I sailed as a "Wiper" in the engine room and with the "black gang." And, it was "below decks" where I went thru the "breaking in" period as the engineer on watch sent me into the "boiler room" for a "bucket of steam" or into the "machine shop" for a left-handed wrench. Eventually, the "hazing" stopped when I began to return with the proper tools such as an "inside caliper" for measuring pipe diameters.

I don't recall any hazing after I "signed on" as a "deck hand" as an "ordinary Seaman" except I seemed to be assigned the unusual jobs: cleaning bilges, butterworthing the fuel tanks or going aloft to change a bulb in the "mast head " light 100 ' above the "main deck" without the use of a safety belt. 90' of the distance was in the seat of a "bos'n's chair"; beyond that I needed to "shimmy" to the top of the "truck," wrestle with the lights corroded "bird cages," remove the "burned out" bulb and replace the new.

On inclement days the "deck gang" would gather in the "shelter deck-mid ships" to perform – at the Bos'n's discretion – "marline-spike seamanship" such as: "whipping small cordage, splicing manila hemp, sewing canvas, making heaving lines and monkey fists, fashioning lanyards, reinforcing bos'n chairs and greasing blocks." "Wire splicing" was left to the bos'n but "deck hands" assisted and learned to wear leather work gloves. Generally, we worked as individuals among groups and listened to "sea stories":

- the oldest "able seaman" was a Norwegian who sailed in four-masted ships, and in brigs, barks and sloops and went to sea for the first time at the age of

seven.
- the bos'n who had been a Chief Petty Officer (CPO) in the US Navy during the war, and who sailed in two oceans at the same time!
- the "ordinary seaman who – in his first trip at sea – was torpedoed in sight of the entrance to the Delaware River off the Jersey/Delaware coast.
- the "able seaman" who was torpedoed off America's eastern coast and was awarded a merchant marine medal for bravery.
- the "quartermaster" of a freighter off Okinawa who kept the ship on a 90° course facing inland during the naval bombardment with shells passing overhead while alongside Marines were disembarking from APAs for the invasion.
- the merchant mariners who felt they should be considered armed forces veterans and entitled to the privileges of the G. I. Bill. Those of us who were "veterans" disagreed reminding them they: avoided the draft, had three square meals each day, slept nightly in a "bunk" with clean sheets and received a bonus when in a war zone and made more money that the most humble G. I.
- at sea there always was the fickle sea: days and nights of rain, high seas broadside and fore and aft, and hurricanes that prevented the ship from "making headway" and the occasional "rogue wave" that "broke over the bow" and over "monkey island" the highest deck about 60' above the "water line."

Fire drills and "abandoned ship" exercises were held once monthly. Lifeboat handling and sailing was held whenever the ship was anchored off shore as in the Gatun

Lake of the Panama Canal or off El-Segundo, CA, while waiting for a berth, or off Suez while waiting for North bound traffic to exit the Suez Canal. It was in these drills that I, and other novice seamen, learned to sail "with the wind."

"Off loading" and "recovering the lifeboat(s)" provided maintenance opportunities for checking the condition and equipment of the lifeboats, greasing the "gravity davits" and "rudder posts," and making certain that each seaman had a "May West" or floating device, and that each was tight and snug to the chest.

There is a myth that sailors don't or can't swim. Well, they better know how to swim if they want to survive with or without a survival vest. It was not unusual for "off watch" sailors to "take a dip."

Anchored off Manhattan at the entrance to the Hudson River several of us put a Jacob's ladder off the port side mid ships and dove off the bow. The flow out of the Hudson was swift and it pushed us toward the ladder, which we would grasp, climb aboard and dive again. Strenuous and dangerous. Had we missed the ladder the current would have sent us "out to sea" and we would have been candidates for rescue by the Coast Guard or worse "lost at sea."

On the Sabine River at Port Arthur, Texas, we dived, once, off the port side, swam under the ship, and headed to the pier. Midway we swam under the keel and another 40' to the dock. Then we realized had we lost our direction we might have had to swim toward the "bow" – 200' + and might have drowned without ever seeing the light of day. We didn't do that again.

In the Gulf of Thailand I was scuba diving with a "buddy." We exited the dive boat on the landside and swam right into a current coming out of a river. We "dove on" a freighter fighting the current and the effort used up a lot of air. By the time I reached the ladder I was exhausted and "out of air." A diver's worst experience. That evening I became nauseous and my toes and fingers "tingled" while heading often for the "head." The first sign of the "bends" or decompression sickness – a killer. And me! certified as a Dive Master by PADI.

Other "underwater" experiences included a stingray ripping my mask and regulator out of my mouth and a less than a perfect and professional dive at the Barrier Reef off Cairns, Australia. That was a real embarrassment! We do learn though, from our experiences – if we survive.

Dives after those and later in life certified me as an Aquanaut for "living and working for twenty-four hours or more in an underwater classroom laboratory at 30'."

In July 1946 the last Marines with less than 85 points for separation from the Marine Corps as World War II veterans departed Taku, China by LST for transfer, at sea, to the USNS *Breckenridge* destined for San Diego.

The *Breckenridge* was a military transport with "hatches" about 15' off the surface of the sea. To transfer from the LST to the transport an improvised "gangway" without railing was positioned between the two ships. One could see that crossing that gangway was going to be perilous for anyone crossing and carrying a "sea bag" on his shoulder. All Marines passing over but one, made it and that Marine, fell into the sea, and was recovered; but, his "sea bag" sank into Davy Jones' Locker at the bottom of the Yellow Sea. Essentially, he had "deep sixed" his wardrobe and his personal items thus departing the ship in San Diego without a thing to his name.

Steaming out of the Port of Boston 24 June 1956 aboard

the SS *Maryland Sun* – Captain A. G. Baldwin, Commanding – and following the coast line, south about 150 miles off shore, we ran into a dense fog. Standing the 8-12 watch on the bow the visibility was nil. Looking aft towards the ship's bridge I could see only blurred port and starboard "running lights" and a hazy white masthead light. I thought: "this is the densest fog I have ever experienced" and it was eerie! Being relieved at midnight, I went aft to the mess hall, grabbed a cup of coffee, and went below to my bunk. I slept with my clothes on, my shoes untied, my weather jacket and life vest nearby. I fell asleep reading *The Young Lions*. At 0630 I was awakened for my next watch and was told by the man on watch that the Italian liner *Andrea Doria* was in a collision east of our position and sinking. When I went to the bridge to "relieve the wheel" I was told by the Captain that the *Andrea Doria* was struck east of our position by the Swedish liner *Stockholm* at 2310 hours. It later sank off New York at 1000 hours 26 June at Latitude 40° 30' north and Longitude 69° 53' west. The Captain was advised by the Coast Guard to stay clear as there were rescue vessels on scene and an oil tanker would be a menace to navigation. That was the only premonition I ever had at sea of possible danger and it caused me to take caution.

The Titanic sails on its maiden voyage out of Southampton. From Batchelor, Six Titanic Paintings Cards © 1998 Dover Publications, Inc.

Forty-four years earlier and in the same approximate geographic zone the British liner *Titanic* collided with an iceberg – on a calm night – at Latitude 49° 56' north and Longitude 41° 43' west at 2140 hours on the 14th of April 1912 and sank the next morning at 0122 hours – 15 April – with the loss of 1500 souls or more.

Above Corpus Christi, Texas, in the bend of the Gulf of Mexico, is Aransas Pass. On the west side of the pass is an oil terminal. Across the bay is the town of Ingleside with a ferry dock and a restaurant. Eating in the restaurant and waiting for the ferry to the terminal it rained "cats and dogs." I saw the ferry pull-in, waited for it to sound its departure whistle and ran out to jump on the stern. Reaching the dockside ramp I realized I made a terrible decision as the ferry was at least six – ten feet away from the dock. The landing was slippery and as I jumped – intending to land on the boat deck – I knew I wasn't going to make it and the next thing I knew I was in the bay. Underwater I could hear the ferries' "emergency whistle" and when I surfaced I heard: "man overboard." Life rings were thrown; I grasped one and was hauled over and pulled to the deck – soaking wet. No unusual comments were made and – after docking – headed to the ship amidst the laughter of my mates.

    I had only one fight at sea. Aboard a foreign destined tanker was a seaman who "pumped iron" and had muscles like Charles Atlas. Underway we got into an argument, which I attempted to avoid by going to my foc'sle. He followed and bullied me and finally he took a swing. I backed off, protected myself from a volley of punches, and noticed he was "muscle bound." Ah! I swung into him, knocked him into a chair, and pummeled him. The next morning the fight was the talk of the mess hall and my "buddy," who was a witness, said: "Moullette you piled into him as if you were getting even with every offense ever bared on you." Perhaps, I was. No trouble from the "iron pumper," progeny of Charles Atlas, after that.

AFTERTHOUGHTS

"Going to sea" is a life experience. In my time at sea I sailed with skippers with little or no formal schooling and with those who had "pick-up" education only and who became skippers thru ship board study and the passing of examinations without "cheat sheets." And, then of course there were those skippers who attended "the academies," such as the United States Maritimes Academy at Kings Point, New York, and who graduated with a bachelor's degree, and a third officer's license. All required continued shipboard study to become second mates, first mates, chief mates, captains, and shipboard pilots for rivers, canals, and ocean ways leading to ports and estuaries. Most shared their knowledge and experiences; others harbored theirs. I preferred the former and one captain recommended me for my first – and only – tour of duty as a bos'n. That was an honor and recognized as such by my shipmates. And, of course it was a tremendous learning experience – supervising and leading experienced sailors, commanding the daily activities of seamen, and being included in shipboard decisions and decision-making.

Those days are behind me for now; but, I yearn for one

more trip – not on a cruise ship or even a liner – where I can feel the wind in my hair and the sea spray in my face. That may not be possible but I keep dreaming as I did when I was a kid. And, who knows, the "fickle finger of fate" may yet point my way.

9 POST WORLD WAR II

Returning from China in the summer of 1946, where I served as a rifleman in Weapons Company, First Battalion, First Marine Regiment of the First Marine Division, I was honorably discharged from the Marine Corps as a Corporal. This rating – after Private and Private First Class and later Lance Corporal – acknowledged that I served as a squad leader in a platoon of 39 men officered by a Lieutenant. Separation from the Marine Corps was at the Great Lakes Naval Training Station, Chicago.

Seeking further adventures I found a job with the Atlantic Refining Company (ARCO) as an ordinary seaman and progressed to able seaman, lifeboatman, and boatswain (bos'n) in three years.

In the summer of 1949 I returned to Temple University High School – Philadelphia – where the University offered accelerated high school courses for veterans who wished to attend college. In one year I completed four high school years and was accepted for admission to the freshman year at Cornell University, Ithaca, New York.

Oh! That "fickle finger of fate," so obvious in my Marine Corps life, pointed at me once again. In the last week of June 1950, as I was completing my high school studies and looking forward to graduation and entering college, the North Koreans invaded South Korea. America went to war, again, and by telegram I was ordered to report to Marine Barracks, Philadelphia Navy Yard – as an "inactive Marine Corps reservist" no later tan 15 July 1950. Graduation had to wait, but I did receive my high school diploma – by mail – on or about mid-June 1951 while on the front lines of the 38th parallel.

The following ensued.

In the fall of 1952 I started my first two years of undergraduate studies at a small southern New Jersey state college now known as Rowan University and in the spring of 1957 I completed my undergraduate studies at the College of New Jersey – formerly the name for Princeton University.

In 1970 I completed my graduate studies at Rutgers – The State University of New Jersey – a masters degree in 1966 and the doctorate in 1970.

Between 1952 and 1970 – while studying and teaching – the sea was still a part of my life. For instance: in my undergraduate years I would return to sea in the summer months to earn money to complete my undergraduate work, to marry, to having a family and eventually to raise five children.

One of those sailings – in 1958 – was aboard the SS *Delaware Sun* for a four-month voyage around the world. This voyage made it possible to place a "down payment" on a new house and a home for my family.

The second – in 1969 – while still engaged in the doctorate program at Rutgers – was in the SS *Bangor* and this voyage allowed me to assemble and organize data I collected to write the doctoral dissertation – the final requirement for the doctors degree. The degree was awarded in June 1970.

The last trip in the SS *Bangor* was the last in my seagoing career as a seaman but not the end of my connection with the "ocean sea."

Between 1979 and 1989, while employed with Arabian American Oil Company (ARAMCO) in Saudi Arabia I was assigned as a technical advisor to assess, plan, initiate and manage maintenance training including marine training aboard the company's many oceangoing tug boats.

For three (3) years prior to employment with ARAMCO I was technical training manager for the Royal Saudi Naval Forces (RSNF) at the Navy's maintenance training center in Damaam. This responsibility was continued after the ARAMCO employment in 1990 and during the first Gulf War.

After the completion of hostilities I returned to the United States and helped in the founding of the Training Ship Tarpon Springs (Florida) and during this time served as a training consultant to the Military Sealift Command (MSC) in Bayonne, New Jersey, prior to the Command's transfer to the U.S. Navy's facility at Norfolk, Virginia.

10 NAVAL INSTITUTE AND OTHER CERTIFICATES

Three naval certificates were issued me. In chronological order they were/are:

The Domain of the Golden Dragon
Issued by the U.S. Naval Institute for crossing the 180th Meridian or the International Date Line. The first crossing was on a troop ship – an APA (attack personnel auxiliary) -- at Latitude 40° 31' North on 23 January 1946 – my 19th birthday. Four crossings followed.

The Golden Shellback
Issued for crossing the Equator aboard the SS *Atlantic States* on 15 December 1947 at Longitude 38° 30' West; this was followed by a returning voyage.

Round the World Circumnavigation of the Globe by Ship
01 July 1958 thru 18 October 1958 aboard the SS *Delaware Sun*.

11 SCUBA DIVING

Working the Mideast for more than 10 years allowed me to scuba dive the Red Sea among shipwrecks and vertical cliffs extending to more than 60' to depth. All dives were within two to three atmospheres which allow a diver to ascend to surface safely. In both the Red Sea and the Persian Gulf, where depths are more shallow, the sea abounds with marine life too numerous to mention. But, it was not unusual to see sharks, moray eels, squid and turtles.

My orientation to scuba diving occurred in a landside pool and in the sea off Tortola Island, British Virgin Islands (BVI). I was "hooked" from the start!

Off the east coast of Arabia – among PADI divers of consequence I earned the following Professional Association of Diving Instructor certificates:

- Scuba Diver
- Open Water Diver
- Deep Water Diver
- Dive Master

In Florida and at the Marine Resources Underwater Lab

at Key West – in April 1990 – I earned the AQUANAUT CERTIFICATE for "living and working for 24 hours or more" and within three atmospheres. Upon surfacing I was medically pronounced healthy, lively and fit. This research dive tested a Chinese diver's theory that "limited amounts of alcohol imbibed under pressure do not contribute to the bends or decompression sickness." The results proved the theory sound.

ANCILLARIES

Prepared for Battle – Unprepared

By John Moullette

Let me put this in perspective. I came out of World War II as a Private First Class in Able Company, First Battalion, First Marines, and out of the occupation of North China as a Corporal in the same outfits of the First Marine Division, Fleet Marine Force (FMF), Pacific.

Seeking further adventure at the age of 19 I sailed in the American Merchant Marine first as an Ordinary Seaman, then as an Able Seaman, and – finally – as a Quartermaster (helmsman) for three years before being recalled to the Marines for the "police action" in Korea.

Departing almost immediately for Korea via the Receiving Station at the Philadelphia Navy Yard, infantry (re-) training at Camp Lejeune, and overseas assembling at Camp Pendleton, I arrived in the Pusan Perimeter by air flights touching down at Honolulu, Wake Island, and Tachikawa, Japan, and then by a train ride to Kobe and a short sea voyage to Korea.

Short on forces "up on the line," I – with many others – was trucked to the front where I joined as a replacement – much to my surprise – A-1-1, where – after a short "snapping in" period – I became a Squad Leader. The fighting against the North Koreans was incessant and continuous and where days fused into nights and nights fused into days with no letup of casualties. I was prepared for this, but not for what was to follow.

Soon after the first of September 1950, I was ordered to

the port of Pusan without explanation and arrived there hoping for an R & R. But, the port was too crowded with Marines – all suffering from fatigue and looking on with "the stare."

After "crapping out" for about an hour, I heard my name called. I answered to a Master Gunnery Sergeant with a clipboard in his hand. Following his verbal command, I – and others – followed him to a beached LST and up the ramp and into a cavernous expanse of LVTs (Landing vehicles tracks) three abreast. The Gunny led us down the rows and called out the numbers and associated personal names. Mine was three port meaning I was assigned to #3 Tractor on the port side of the LST facing forward.

Somewhat confused, I shouted out and asked the Gunny: "When is my squad, still at the front, coming on board?" He replied: "I don't know what you mean; you are assigned to this tractor as the driver." I replied: "You've got to be kidding" as I had never driven an LVT and went ashore at Okinawa on an LCI (landing craft infantry) sometimes called a Higgins Boat. There was much laughter among the men as the Gunny insisted I was listed with an MOS (military occupation specialist) of such and such a number. I was astounded! "How could that be? I had always been a grunt," I said. And, the Gunny said: "Here it is in black and white," with continuous laughter among my future shipmates on the LST.

Then it dawned on me – coming through the Receiving Station at Philadelphia, the "guidance sergeant" asked my civilian occupation and I responded: "Able Seaman – Quartermaster." Undoubtedly, he thumbed through his military dictionary of occupational titles and equated it with – amphibious tractor driver. The Gunny saw no ifs, ands, or buts about it and LVT-3-Port became my tractor.

Fortunately, others in the crowd were trained as amphibious tractor drivers at Camp Del Mar and they took it upon themselves to train me in an accelerated fashion. Sitting in the left seat, I was instructed how to "power-up" and how to drive forward – just a few feet – by braking left and braking right and how to put it in reverse – doing the same thing again and again – not in the water or on land – but at sea while the LST was underway.

With Marines from the front we were headed for what was to become the landing at Inchon. With naval ships pounding the coast with artillery, the landing Marines were loaded into the LVTs – 30 to mine. My heart was in my stomach and other parts of my anatomy were tight. I had the lives of 30 plus Marines in my hands.

The red landing light went off, the yellow light came on for an indeterminable amount of time with sweat running down my face and elsewhere. Then came the green light and the AMTRACs on the portside of the LST started to move. I released the brakes and rolled in controlled fashion – down the deck and down the ramp and into the water. I wasn't prepared for the instant sinking of the tractor; sea water appeared over the peep sight and water from an open bilge port poured in – ankle deep for the 30 Marines, who began to scream. "Christ," I thought, "I'm going to drown us all." In one quick motion the AMTRAC bobbed to the surface, the tracks caught the friction of the water, and the tractor was moving forward right behind LVT-2-Port, and the screaming stopped when the Assistant Driver and machine gunner announced "all is well and the bilge port is closed."

I had been briefed with others that after departing the LST we had no more than 60 minutes to make it to the beach as the tide would go out and we would be stranded and subject to enemy small arms fire and artillery bombardments.

I felt the tracks grasp the sand and the gravel of the beach and I moved the tractor along until the beach master motioned me to the left of LVT-2 and then brought me horizontally in line with other tractors and signaled me to stop.

The third man of LVT-2 lowered the ramp in the rear and 30 Marines poured out to the left and right of the tractor and formed a defensive position facing inland and the possible onslaught from the North Koreans. "My Marines" followed.

Turning the engines off and "shutting down," I exited the tractor, looked out on the sea to see several tractors bogged down in the mud flats, and I turned my attention to the "perimeter." The Marines were "hunkered down" and the perimeter was secure. LVT-3-Port was in a defensive position and its machine gun manned. The next morning – at early dawn – the Marines moved forward and LVT-3-Port and other tractors followed providing the necessary covering fire.

Finally, a break came for chow and I was able to reflect on a battle I was unprepared for – getting 30 men ashore, safely.

JOHN B. MOULLETTE, Ed. D.
Consultant
Maritime Training

Consultant to Military Sealift Command – Atlantic (MSCLANT), Headquarters, Bayonne, NJ, 31 March thru 10 May 1996.

- Studied, evaluated, and rated United States Navy Education and Training Documents (NAVEDTRAD) in Basic Shipboard Firefighting, Helicopter Firefighting, and Shipboard Damage Control against recognized Instructional Systems Development (ISD) standards for conformance and levels of instructional difficulty at the Afloat Personnel Management Center, Bayonne, NJ, 01 April thru 08 April 1996. Evaluations and ratings CONFIDENTIAL.
- Observed, evaluated, and rated naval trained instructors in the delivery of subject content instruction against established terminal, enabling, and performance objectives as recorded in subject NAVEDTRA documents in relation to ISD standards for conformance in the training of Civilian Mariners at the MSCLANT Fire Training School, Naval Weapons Station, Earle, NJ, 09 April thru 22 April 1996. Evaluations and ratings CONFIDENTIAL.
- Observed, evaluated, and rated randomly selected groups of Civilian Mariners in emergency drills for performance capabilities measured against training objectives, instructor delivery, and shipboard job descriptions for emergencies aboard the USNS

COMFORT (T-AH20) – a hospital ship – at sea and in support of Military Readiness Evaluation (MRE), 23 April thru 19 May 1996. Evaluations and ratings CONFIDENTIAL.

14 May 1996
Tarpon Springs, Florida

John B. Moullette

USNS *Comfort* (T-AH 20)
Military Sealift Command

Hull .... Converted San Clemente Class Supertanker (SS Rose City)
Propulsion ... Main Engine Steam, Single Screw Geared Steam Turbine
Length .... 894 feet
Beam .... 105 feet, 9 inches
Design Draft .... 32 feet, 9 inches
Full Load Displacement .... 69,360 long tons
Flight Deck .... one spot
Endurance .... 13,420 nautical miles
Speed .... 17.5 knots
Shaft Horse Power 24,000
JP5 Capacity .... 31,080 gallons
DFM Capacity .... 1,779,624 gallons
Distillers (4) .... 75,000 GPD
Fresh Water Storage 350,180
A/C Plants (3) .... 400 tons each
Auxiliary Diesel Generators (3) .... 2,000 KW
Emergency Diesel Generator (1) .... 1,500 KW
Crew Size:
    USNS Comfort Civilian Mariners .... ROS:13 .... FOS:62
    Embarked MTF Navy Military Personnel .... ROS:44 ..... FOS: 1,200
Acquisition/Conversion/Initial Outfitting Cost .... $514 million
Converted by ..... National Steel & Shipbuilding Co., San Diego, Calif.
Ship Sponsor .... Mrs. William M. Narva
Naming Ceremony .... Aug. 15, 1987
Delivered to U.S. Navy .... Dec. 1, 1987

EMBARKED MEDICAL TREATMENT FACILITY
(MTF) CAPABILITIES

    The Medical Treatment Facility aboard USNS Comfort is one of the largest trauma facilities in the United States and offers a full spectrum of surgical and medical services. Patients arrive aboard primarily by helicopter and sometimes by small boat. After being assessed for medical treatment in casualty reception, patients are routed either to surgery or other services depending on the severity of their wounds or medical condition. They would be admitted to one of 16 wards.

    Total Bed Capacity 1,000
    Intensive Care Beds 80

APPENDICES

THE *YOUNG AMERICA*

The Author's first troop ship

S. S. YOUNG AMERICA
XAP Attack Troop Transport
World War II   -   Pacific

John B. Moullette

U.S. Department of Homeland Security
United States Coast Guard

Director
National Vessel Documentation Center

792 T J Jackson Drive
Falling Waters, WV 25419-9502
Staff Symbol: NVDC
Phone: (304) 271-2400
Fax: (304) 271-2405
Email: Kim.E.Demory@uscg.mil

16713/28 R
FOIA 08-0647
March 22, 2008

John Moullette
3937 Winding Road North
Fort Garland, CO 81133

Dear Mr. Moullette:

This is in response to your letter received March 17, 2008 requesting documentation information on the vessel S.S. YOUNG AMERICA.

A search was conducted in our database. We were unable to associate the vessel name S.S. YOUNG AMERICA with any vessels in our database. We also searched the Merchant Vessels of the United States Books and we were unable to associate the name S.S. YOUNG AMERICA with any vessels in the books.

If you have any additional information that may be helpful in identifying the vessel such as the official number please send your request to the above address.

If you have any questions, you may contact me at (800) 799-8362.

Sincerely,

Kim E Demory

Kim E. Demory
Records and Research Manager
Data Management & Administration Division
By direction

Nearly five years after receiving the above letter _ 21 February 2013 _ I contacted the sender, by e-mail with the following finding:

The S.S. young America was a C2 cargo/troopship built in 1943 by the Moore Dry Dock Co., and operated by the Mississippi Shipping Co. It was 459 feet long with a beam of 63 feet and did 16 knots. Its cargo space was 119,000 cubic feet and carried 1500 Marines one of which was me. Your letter shows no available data on this ship. This data was revealed in a memoir by a Navy veteran who served in her as a radioman.

Please see Bibliography.

SS *ATLANTIC STATES*

The Author's first oil tanker

The *Atlantic States* was my first merchant ship and I always will have strong feelings for her and for the officers and men I sailed with. They taught me all I know about sailing and all I know about seamanship. They, also, added to my knowledge of life and the ways and means of people.

SHIPMATES

SS *Atlantic States*, outbound from Philadelphia 1946 1947

The author (left) with an unidentified shipmate.

down to the sea again, again and again

Gig Bonitatis, the bos'n, and the author.

Unidentified shipmate and the author

SIN-BAD THE SAILOR

The author.

The author.

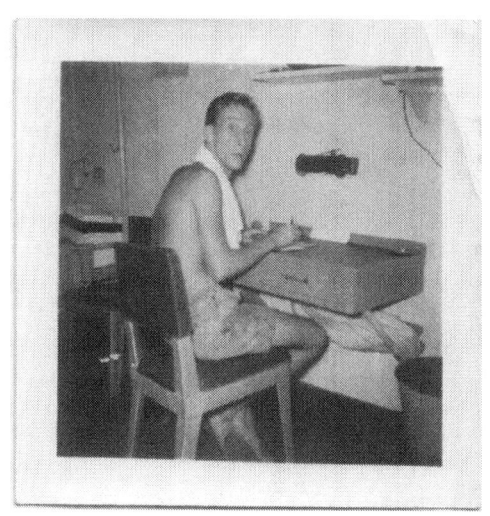

The author at his desk.

The author, off Manhattan, NY

John B. Moullette

VESSEL DOCUMENTATION FOR THE SS *ATLANTIC STATES*

National Vessel Documentation Center
Attn: Ms. Jennifer R. Barney
       Records and Research Assistant
792 T.J. Jackson Drive
Falling Waters, WV 25419-9502

Ms. Jennifer R. Barney:

Thank you for returning my call last Friday and for your letter and materials of nearly three (3) years ago (9/17/2004). A copy is enclosed.

With respect to my recent phone request, I have decided to limit my research and focus on one (1) ship that was in Atlantic Refining Company's fleet between the years 1945 and 1952 inclusively. That ship, a tanker, is/was the SS Atlantic States. The specific information requested is:
- hull or construction number
- name of the shipyard where built and, perhaps, the city and state
- date of construction and/or launching; and,
- the vessel's official number

Here is a dilemma: prior to 1946, inclusive, the official number of the Atlantic States was 240036 and there after it became 243036. (Merchant Vessels of the United States -- Index of Managing Owners).

Perhaps there is a reason _ on record _ for this change which you might share.

Other data relative to the Atlantic States that would be helpful is:
- overall length of the ship
- breadth (width) of the ship
- the ship's displacement tonnage; and,
- the draft of the vessel

Again, thank you for your assistance _ past and present _ and I look forward to hearing from you.

John B. Moullette

719-379-4611
jhnmoul@aol.com

down to the sea again, again and again

```
Form No. 1319              TREASURY DEPARTMENT - BUREAU OF CUSTOMS
  (July 1941)
                              APPROVAL OF HOME PORT OF VESSEL

Commissioner of Customs,              PORT    Philadelphia, Pa.
Treasury Department,
Bureau of Customs                              January 4       , 19 43
Washington, D. C.

SIR:
        In accordance with the provisions of the Act of February 16, 1925, I hereby designate
                    Philadelphia, Pa.
a port of documentation, as the home port of the    Electric (Steam) Screw
                                                    (Rig and name of vessel)
          ATLANTIC STATES                , official number  2 4 3 0 3 6
                                                            K K O Y - signal
and request your approval thereof.

                                    Respectfully,
                                         The Atlantic Refining Company
                                              A. W. Garrebrant
                                         [signature]       Vice President
                                                            Owner
                        Please type or print name above signature and cross off inappropriate designation below it.

FORWARDED  A. RAYMOND RAFF  COLLECTOR    APPROVAL:
    BY   [signature]                         Commissioner of Customs
   L. M. King,   Act. Dy.                 The  [struck out]  hereby approves the home port desig-
   Port: Philadelphia, Pa.                nated. Confirming approval by telephone on
                                          March 2, 1943, at 12:12 PM, EWT.
   Date: March 2, 1943.

   Remarks: NEW VESSEL: Philadelphia, Pa.    J. W. Gulick, Jr.
   approved as home port and official       Acting Assistant Deputy Commissioner
   No. 243036 & Signal letters K K O Y                March 3, 1943.
   awarded by the Bureau by telephone                    (Date)
   March 2, 1943 at 12.12PM(EWT)

   If the owner is a corporation, the name of the corporation should be typed in, followed by the signature of a corporate officer
or of a duly authorized agent as the case may be. If the owner is a firm, the firm name should be typed in, followed by the
signature of one of the members of the firm. His capacity should be indicated by the words "member of firm." In case of
joint ownership, all the owners should sign the application or one designated as managing owner may sign as such.
   In case of a partnership the name of such partnership should be typed in in full, followed by the signature of one of the
partners. He should sign as "co-partner."

                            U. S. GOVERNMENT PRINTING OFFICE   16—24504-1
```

John B. Moullette

THE ATLANTIC REFINING COMPANY
PETROLEUM PRODUCTS
260 SOUTH BROAD STREET
PHILADELPHIA, PA.

HARRY G. SCHAD
GENERAL MANAGER TRANSPORTATION DEPARTMENT
CABLE ADDRESS: BRIDGE, PHILADELPHIA

January 13, 1943

S. S. "ATLANTIC STATES"

Collector of Customs
Philadelphia, Pa.

Attention: Mr. King

Dear Sir:

This vessel is now completing building at the Sun Shipyard and Dry Dock Company Plant, Chester, Pa., and is expected to be ready for operation in about two weeks' time. When ready to sail, vessel will be immediately requisitioned by War Shipping Administration.

Enclosed herewith please find Application for Approval of Home Port of this vessel executed in triplicate and Owner's Application for Official Number executed in duplicate.

Even though the vessel has not yet been measured by your Admeasurers, we would appreciate your applying to Washington promptly for the official number, by telephone at our expense, if it can be arranged. We are most anxious to obtain the vessel's official number so that we can make application for radio license and other documents.

Yours very truly,

THE ATLANTIC REFINING COMPANY

Vice President

down to the sea again, again and again

Certificate No. _____

THE UNITED STATES OF AMERICA
UNITED STATES CUSTOMS SERVICE

Issued subject to approval by
Bureau of Customs
Treasury Department

Port of __Philadelphia__

__March 1__, 19__43__.

CERTIFICATE OF ADMEASUREMENT

I CERTIFY that an admeasurement has been made of the **electric screw** called the __ATLANTIC STATES__ of __PHILADELPHIA, PA.__, official number _____ which was built by __Sun Shipbuilding & Dry Dock Company__ in the year 19__43__, at __Chester__, State of __Pennsylvania__, of __steel__; and has been known as builder's hull No. __230__; that she has __one__ deck, __two masts and two kingposts__ mast, __raked__ stem, and __elliptical__ stern; that her register length is __45__ 1/__ feet, her register breadth is __65__ 2/__ feet, her register depth is __36__ 8/__ feet, her height under upper deck is _____ feet,

and that her tonnage is as follows:

	TONS	100THS
Capacity under tonnage deck	7483	55
Capacity between decks, above tonnage deck		
Capacity of enclosures on the upper deck, viz:		
Forecastle 37.47, bridge _____, poop 255.08, trunks 1.85		
deckhouses 568.46, side houses _____, chart house _____		
radio house _____, excess hatchways _____, light and air 139.69	1053	55
GROSS TONNAGE	8537	10
Deductions under Section 4153, Revised Statutes, as amended (Section 77, title 46, United States Code):		
Crew space 561.61, master's cabin 22.46, steering gear _____		
anchor gear 7.86, boatswains' stores 85.37, chart house 13.63		
donkey engine (ballast pump) 19.12, radio house 7.91		
storage of sails _____, propelling power (actual space 1116.24) 32% gross 2731.87		
TOTAL DEDUCTIONS	3449	83
NET TONNAGE	5087	

The following-described spaces, and no others, have been omitted, viz:
Forepeak __32.01__, afterpeak __11.17__, other spaces (except double bottoms) for water ballast _____; open forecastle __63.77__, open bridge __211.20__, open poop _____, open shelter deck _____, cabins _____ companions __19.69__, galley __17.49__, skylights __12.10__, wheelhouse __19.59__, water-closets __58.00__; anchor gear __8.90__, condenser _____, donkey boiler __3.08__, steering gear __19.10__, light and air spaces, including skylights, over propelling machinery __154.48__, other machinery spaces __75.50__, lookout houses _____

_____ Admeasurer. (SEAL) _____ Collector of Customs.

I agree to the above description and admeasurement.

_____ Agent.

65

John B. Moullette

Form 1320
(May 1941)

APPLICATION OF OWNER FOR OFF. L. NUMBER
(46 CFR 1.15 AND 1.48)
TREASURY DEPARTMENT — BUREAU OF CUSTOMS

To the Collector of Customs.

Sir: Application is hereby made, in accordance with section 4177, Revised Statutes, and regulations established pursuant thereto, for an OFFICIAL NUMBER for the following-described vessel, which is ready for marine documents:

Rig, **Elec. (Steam Screw**; number of decks, **1**; number of masts, **2 & 2 kingposts**

Name, **ATLANTIC STATES**

Gross tonnage, **8537.10**; net tonnage, **5087**

Register dimensions: Length, **451 7/10**; breadth, **65 2/10**; depth, **36 8/10**

Material of hull, **Steel**; hull No. **230**; horsepower, **5000**

Stem, **Raked**; stern, **Elliptical**

Builder, **Sun Shipbuilding & Dry Dock Co.**

When begun, **September 9, 1942**; when launched, **December 31, 1942**

When built, **1943**; where built, **Chester, Pa.**

Engine: Type **Turbo-Electric**
Built by **General Electric Company** at **Lynn, Mass**, in **1942**

Bureau Form 1319, application for approval of designated home port, must be executed in duplicate and accompany this application.

Owner, **Atlantic Refining Company**; address, **260 So. Broad St., Philadelphia, Pa.**

Service, **Tank**; number of officers, **8**; crew, **70 (Incl. Gun Crew)**

Signal letters? **Yes**; equipped with radio transmitting apparatus? **Yes**

Philadelphia, Pa. approved as home port and Off. No. 243036 & Signal letters KKOY awarded by the Bureau by telephone March 2, 1943 at 12.12PM(EWT)

Respectfully,
The Atlantic Refining Company
Vice President

Commissioner of Customs
Treasury Department,
Bureau of Customs
Washington, D. C.

Port of **Philadelphia, Pa.**
Collector's Office, **March 2, 1943**

Sir: I transmit herewith the application for assignment of an OFFICIAL NUMBER for the vessel described above.

Respectfully,
A. RAYMOND RAFE, COLLECTOR
By
A. Dy.
Collector of Customs.

down to the sea again, again and again

TREASURY DEPARTMENT
BUREAU OF CUSTOMS
WASHINGTON

OFFICE OF THE COMMISSIONER

ADDRESS REPLY TO
COMMISSIONER OF CUSTOMS

IN REPLY REFER TO

March 3, 1943.

The Collector of Customs,

Philadelphia, Pa.

Sir:

The receipt is acknowledged of Form 1319 designating your port as the home port of the electric (steam) screw ATLANTIC STATES (243036).

It is noted that A. A. Garrabrant, as vice president of The Atlantic Refining Company, has executed the application. Your attention is invited to the footnote at the bottom of this form to the effect that the corporate name must be signed by a corporate officer or a duly authorized agent. As the vice president is not such a corporate officer as may designate home ports without special authority, he may not execute this application unless there is on file in your office an authorization from the corporation to do so.

Form 1319 is returned herewith in order that the designation "authorized agent" may be inserted under the vice president's name, if a proper authorization is on file in your office. Otherwise, it will be necessary to secure proper authorization and to execute a new form or the designation of home port will not be approved unless made by another person having authority.

Very truly yours,

Henry E. Sweet
Assistant Deputy Commissioner

Enclosure
No. 71989

FOR DEFENSE
BUY
UNITED
STATES
SAVINGS
BONDS
AND STAMPS

John B. Moullette

STEAM AND MOTOR VESSELS

For steam and motor vessels of 100 gross tons and over, the following additional information should be given.

Cruising speed, _____ knots; full speed, 14.50 knots; cruising radius, 9650 nautical miles.
Fuel ordinarily used, if fitted for burning both coal and oil, 011

Fuel capacity (fill in applicable spaces only):
 Bunker coal (allow 42 cubic feet to ton of 2,240 pounds) None _____ tons.
 Bunker oil (231 cubic inches to gallon, or 1 cubic foot = 7.48 gallons) 236,800 _____ gallons.
 Bunker gasoline (231 cubic inches to gallon, or 1 cubic foot = 7.48 gallons) None _____ gallons.

Daily consumption (24 hours) at cruising speed:
 Coal _____ ---- _____ tons of 2,240 pounds.
 Oil _____ 8520 _____ gallons.
 Gasoline _____ ---- _____ gallons.

Forepeak tank _____ Water Ballast
Afterpeak tank _____ " "
Side tanks _____ Wing & Center Cargo Tanks   Write on each line "Water ballast", "Oil fuel", or other object for which space is
Double bottom _____ Feed Water   provided—or "No" if space is not in use.

Draft, Loaded, 28'11-7/8" feet; in ballast, 19'0" feet.
Dead-weight capacity:¹ 13450 tons of 2,240 pounds.
Passenger capacity: Cabin passengers _____ - _____, other passengers² _____ - _____; total _____ -
Tankage capacity (exclusive of bunkers) _____ 4,640,000 _____ gallons.
Refrigerator capacity: Number of chambers _____ - _____; total insulated cargo space _____ - _____ cubic feet.
Radio set: Type, R. C. A. , transformer input, 1/2 kw.; auxiliary power Storage Battery
                (Marconi, R. & C., etc.)   (Storage battery or gas engine)

Fill in appropriate spaces only for above-required data.

¹ The weight required to depress the vessel from the light water-line (only the machinery and equipment on board) to the load-line.
² Third cabin and steerage.

[This oath should be taken if the vessel described in the application was not built during the present or preceding year.]

State of _____ }
County of _____ } ss.:

I, _____ of _____,
managing owner of the _____, called the _____,
do solemnly swear that this vessel has not borne an official number and/or
or any other name.

Subscribed and sworn to before me this _____ day of _____

[L. S.] MAR 3 1943

down to the sea again, again and again

Customs Form 1321
TREASURY DEPARTMENT
46 U. S. C. 3, 45 ; 46 C. F. R.
L.16, 1.17, 16.30 (c)
May 1942

3-39373

NOTICE TO OWNER OR MASTER OF AWARD OF OFFICIAL NUMBER AND SIGNAL LETTERS

UNITED STATES CUSTOMS SERVICE
WASHINGTON, D. C.

COLLECTOR OF CUSTOMS
MAR 9 - 1943
CUSTOM HOUSE
PHILADELPHIA

Date March 8, 1943.

SIR: Under authority of R. S. 4177, as amended (46 U. S. C. 45), Section 3 of the Act of July 5, 1884, as amended (46 U. S. C. 3), and Executive Order No. 9083 (7 F. R. 1609), the following official number and visual signal letters (if requested) have been awarded the vessel described below:

No. 243036   SIGNAL LETTERS K K O Y

Rig El. s. (steam)   Home port Philadelphia, Pa.

Name ATLANTIC STATES

Tonnage 8,537 gross, 5,087 net.   Horsepower, if a machinery-propelled vessel 5,000

When built 1943   Where built Chester, Pa.

In case the above description is erroneous in any respect, you will please notify this office at once. Otherwise, the official number above shall be permanently marked on the main beam of your vessel.

By direction of the Commissioner:

(Signed) I. W. Gulick, Jr.

Acting *Assistant Deputy Commissioner.*

The Collector of Customs,
Philadelphia, Pa.

LAW OFFICES
CARDILLO & SMITH

JOSEPH CARDILLO, JR.
DANIEL L. SMITH, JR.
CURRAN C. TIFFANY

DIGBY 4-0484
CABLE ADDRESS: AVOCARD, N.Y.

52 BROADWAY, NEW YORK 4, N.Y.

May 8, 1956

Collector of Customs
Philadelphia 6, Penna.

Attention of Mr. Jack Slotter

Re: S/T Atlantic States
Official No. 234036

Dear Sirs:

We represent Winco Tankers, Inc., a corporation which is under contract to purchase the above vessel from The Atlantic Refining Company.

The closing of title is scheduled for Thursday, May 10, 1956. In this connection we would very much appreciate your issuing and sending to the Collector of Customs at Wilmington, Delaware, an abstract of the title record of the vessel.

We enclose herewith a check to the order of the Collector of Customs in the amount of $1.00, which we understand is the fee for issuing such an abstract. If any additional expense or fee is involved, we shall be happy to pay it.

With appreciation for your cooperation, we are

Respectfully yours,

CARDILLO & SMITH

By Curran Tiffany
Curran C. Tiffany

CCT:cm
Enclosure

down to the sea again, again and again

TREASURY DEPARTMENT
3.30, 3.31, C. R.
June 1934

CERTIFICATE OF OWNERSHIP OF VESSEL

BUREAU OF CUSTOMS

PORT OF __Philadelphia, Pa.__

COLLECTOR'S OFFICE __May 10, 1956__

I hereby certify that, according to the records of this office, the __Electric Screw__ called the __ATLANTIC STATES__, of this port, official number __243036__, tonnage __8525__ gross, __5699__ net, built at __Chester, Pa.__ in 19__43__, and last documented at __Philadelphia, Pa.__ on __Feb. 14, 1954__ (P.E. No. __217__) is owned as follows:

_____The Atlantic Refining Company_____
_____260 South Broad Street, Philadelphia, Pa._____
_____Incorporated under the laws of the State of Pennsylvania_____
_____Sole owner_____

; and that there are on record in this office * __No__ mortgages, liens, or other encumbrances:

Given under my hand and seal of office this __10th__ day of __May__, 19__56__.

[IMPRESS SEAL]

Hon. Fred G. Return, Collector of Customs A. M.

By: __Jack Slotter, Acting__ Deputy Collector.

Minimum fee. $1.00.

U-BOAT ACTIONS IN THE ATLANTIC

For Americans, World War II began with the Japanese bombing of Pearl Harbor – 07 December 1941 – and the crippling of America's Pacific Fleet in Hawaii. Forty-four days later – 23 January 1942 – I turned 15 and too young to enter any of the armed forces including American's merchant navy more commonly referred to as the Merchant Marine.

Sailing from Bremen on the Baltic and from St. Nazaire on the French occupied west coast, German U-boats headed west across the Atlantic Ocean to strike at the privately owned ships – freighters and tankers – of America's manufacturing industry. The U-boats were successful for the first 18 months and less successful for the remainder of the war in Europe which ended 07 May 1945.

The carnage along New Jersey's coastal shores was very visible to anyone who visited the Jersey shore. My parents and I were able to observe the debris: oil spills, freight, life jackets, oars, lifeboats (stacked and damaged) and flotsam from American industries that had been headed east to England with supplies. A newspaper reported that in one month – February 1942 – more than 200 merchant ships had been sunk with the loss of 9000 or more merchant seamen. To German submarines these days were known as "the happy days."

One of the ships – outbound for England – was the SS *Meriwether Lewis*, which was torpedoed and sunk with no survivors on 02 March 1943. A family friend was on board: Harry J. Mote, Jr., second engineer. The war became more close to the citizens and families of Camden, New Jersey.

Another ship was the SS *Atlantic States*.

The German Enigma codes had been captured – early in the war – and interpreted by the Allies. And, the Americans generally knew the locations of all U-boats on the seas and especially those in the western Atlantic. One of those was the U-857, which was in the vicinity of the *Atlantic States* 05 April 1945. The ship was struck by a torpedo presumably fired by U-857 off the Jersey coast; the torpedo did not explode and the Atlantic States sailed safely on to its next port of call for repairs. The US Navy reported the submarine as "probably sunk" with all hands.

Approximately 18 months later with the war over and after my separation from the Marine Corps, I signed aboard the *Atlantic States* and shipped in her for the next two years. In that period of time and never after did anyone tell me the *States* had been hit by a torpedo which did not explode. Much later in life I read <u>Shadow Divers</u> by Robert Kurson (see Bibliography). It is the story of two scuba divers from Brielle on the Jersey coast who dived on what they presumed to be the U-857. Finding no definitive markings they perused through American, British and German archives and continuous diving – most of it hazardous – to learn it was the U-869 and not the U-857 that was in the path of the SS *Atlantic States* on the spring morning of 05 April 1945. The U-boat's roster is attached.

U.S. Ships Sunk or Damaged on Eastcoast of U.S. and Gulf of Mexico During World War II

Date　Ship　Type　Cause　Result　Location　Deaths

Eastcoast of U.S. (174 ships)

Eastcoast of U.S. 1941 (2 ships)

Date	Ship	Type	Cause	Result	Location	Deaths
12/10/41	Oregon (States Steamship)	Freighter	Collision	Sunk	Eastcoast	Crew 17
12/26/41	Nancy Moran	Tug	Collision	Sunk	Eastcoast	Unknown

Eastcoast of U.S. 1942 (121 ships)

Date	Ship	Type	Cause	Result	Location	Deaths
01/08/42	General Richard Arnold (USAT)	Mine planter	Capsized	Sunk	Eastcoast	Crew 8 or 10
01/14/42	Brazos	Freighter	Collision	Sunk	Eastcoast	None
01/17/42	San Jose	Freighter	Torpedo and Collision	Sunk	Eastcoast	None
01/17/42	Santa Elisa	Freighter	Collision	Damaged	Eastcoast	None
01/18/42	Allan Jackson	Tanker	Torpedo	Sunk	Eastcoast	Crew 22
01/18/42	Malay	Tanker	Torpedo & Shelled	Damaged	Eastcoast	Crew 4
01/19/42	City of Atlanta	Freighter	Torpedo	Sunk	Eastcoast	Crew 43
01/22/42	Norvana	Freighter	Torpedo	Sunk	Eastcoast	Crew 29
01/22/42	Olympic	Tanker (Panama)	Torpedo	Sunk	Eastcoast	Crew 31
01/23/42	Venore	Collier	Torpedo & Shelled	Sunk	Eastcoast	Crew 17
01/25/42	Olney	Tanker	Shelled [7 torpedoes missed]	Damaged	Eastcoast	None
01/26/42	West Ivis	Freighter	Torpedo	Sunk	Eastcoast	Crew 36; AG 9
01/27/42	Francis E. Powell	Tanker	Torpedo	Sunk	Eastcoast	Crew 4
01/27/42	Halo	Tanker	Shelled	Damaged	Eastcoast	None
01/30/42	Rochester	Tanker	Torpedo & Shelled	Sunk	Eastcoast	Crew 4
02/02/42	W. L. Steed	Tanker	Torpedo & Shelled	Sunk	Eastcoast	Crew 34
02/03/42	San Gil	Freighter (Panama)	Torpedo & Shelled	Sunk	Eastcoast	Crew 2
02/04/42	India Arrow	Tanker	Torpedo & Shelled	Sunk	Eastcoast	Crew 26
02/05/42	China Arrow	Tanker	Torpedo	Sunk	Eastcoast	None

http://www.usmm.org/eastgulf.html　　　　　　　　8/28/2004

down to the sea again, again and again

02/05/45	Clio	Tanker (Panama)	Collision/Fire	salvaged Damaged	Eastcoast	Unknown
02/05/45	Spring Hill	Tanker	Collision/Fire	Damaged	Eastcoast	Crew 9; AG 11
03/08/45	Benjamin R. Milam	Liberty	Explosion	Sunk-salvaged	Eastcoast	Unknown
04/05/45	Atlantic States	Tanker	Torpedo	Damaged	Eastcoast	None
04/05/45	Captain Nathaniel B. Palmer	Fishing boat	Depth charge	Sunk	Eastcoast	Crew 3
04/18/45	Swiftscout	Tanker	Torpedo	Sunk	Eastcoast	Crew 1
04/23/45	John Carver	Liberty	Explosion during repairs	Total loss	Eastcoast	Unknown
05/05/45	Black Point	Collier	Torpedo	Sunk	Eastcoast	Crew 11; AG 1
08/24/45	Marguerite Le Hand	Freighter	Collision	Unknown	Eastcoast	Unknown
10/17/45	Joshua W. Alexander	Liberty	Grounded	Damaged	Eastcoast	Unknown
10/21/45	Medford	Fishing trawler	Collision	Sunk	Eastcoast	Crew 7
10/21/45	Thomas H. Barry (USAT)	Troopship	Collision	Damaged	Eastcoast	None
12/31/45	R. S. Wilson	Liberty	Grounded	Total loss	Eastcoast	Unknown

✓ (Atlantic States row) — U Boat 8-69

Eastcoast of U.S. 1946 (3 ships)

04/02/46	Charles S. Haight	Liberty	Grounded	Total loss	Eastcoast	Unknown
06/25/46	Gold Creek	Tanker	Grounded	Damaged	Eastcoast	Unknown
08/05/46	Homestead	Tanker	Lightning & fire	Total loss	Eastcoast	Unknown

Gulf of Mexico (46 ships)

Gulf of Mexico 1942 (42 ships)

02/19/42	Pan Massachusetts	Tanker	Torpedo	Sunk	GulfMexico	Crew 20
03/11/42	Halo	Tanker	Torpedo	Damaged	GulfMexico	None
05/04/42	Joseph M. Cudahy	Tanker	Torpedo	Sunk	GulfMexico	Crew 27
05/04/42	Munger T. Ball	Tanker	Torpedo & machine-gunned	Sunk	GulfMexico	Crew 30
05/04/42	Norlindo	Freighter	Torpedo	Sunk	GulfMexico	Crew 5

http://www.usmm.org/eastgulf.html   8/28/2004

Kommandant: KptLt. Helmut Neuerburg
am 28.2.1945 im Mittelatlantik auf 34°30' N und 08°13' W versenkt

FkMt	Bienentreu	Mathias	04.12.21
MaschMt	Böhm	Otto	30.03.23
OLt	Brandt	Siegfried	19.06.22
MaschOGfr	Breit	Wilhelm	18.12.24
MaschOGfr	Brems	Ewald	25.03.24
MechGfr	Brizius	Otto	25.02.26
MaschMt	Dagg	Fritz	28.01.20
MaschOGfr	Dietmayer	Eduard	30.01.25
MaschGfr	Dietz	Hans	17.05.25
MaschMt	Dölcher	Karl	27.07.21
OBtsMt	Drabhoff	Walter	18.06.20
MaschOGfr	Dreyer	Karl-Heinz	13.09.24
MtrHGfr	Eder	Max	08.08.22
MaschMt	Eigenbrodt	Karl	27.12.21
MarSt Arzt Dr.	Esau	Ernst-Christian	28.12.13
FkOGfr	Gehlsen	Richard	20.10.24
MaschOGfr	Geißel	Otto	28.03.25
MaschOGfr	Geratzki	Gerhard	13.02.25
MechGfr	Gradl	Kurt	29.04.25
BtsMt	Grosser	Helmut	30.03.23
MechHGfr	Grunert	Hugo	01.10.19
MechOGfr	Häselbarth	Karl	06.02.22
MtrOGfr	Haun	Erwin	04.05.22
OMasch	Hentschel	Arthur	13.10.18
MaschOGfr	Hirsch	Horst	04.04.25
MtrGfr	Hitze	Heinz	04.02.25
FkMstr	Horenburg	Martin	01.10.19
OLt (Ing)	Keßler	Ludwig	10.06.13
MtrHGfr	Kischka	Rafael	25.09.19
OMasch	Koch	Robert	06.09.13
MaschOGfr	Kornweih	Helmut	29.01.24
MechMt	Kühnhold	Oskar	28.02.23
OStrm	Lenk	Heinz	08.02.17
Mtr	Mehlig	Paul	21.09.19
FkOGfr	Mehnert	Rolf	19.08.24
MtrOGfr	Meineke	Georg	14.04.25
MaschMt	Mocker	Erich	01.06.23
MtrOGfr	Moosmann	Fritz	15.06.25
MtrOGfr	Nedel	Franz	22.08.24
KptLt	Neuerburg	Helmut	25.08.17
MaschOGfr	Nolte	Willi	23.10.24
MtrGfr	Oßwald	Heinz	07.10.25
BtsMt	Plath	Leo	04.08.19
MtrOGfr	Reber	Hans-Georg	09.05.21
MaschOGfr	Rothsprak	Willi	26.01.21
MtrOGfr	Schnick	Willy	05.11.25
MtrOGfr	Seefeldt	Willi	18.04.19
OStrm	Stockhorst	Wilhelm	01.10.20
MaschOGfr	Tabel	Wilhelm	07.02.23
MaschOGfr	Tölke	Erich	06.10.10
FkOGfr	Uhlarsch	Johann	23.05.25
OMaschMt	Verhülsdonk	Heinrich	01.02.20
MaschOGfr	Voigt	Heinz	05.04.23
MtrOGfr	Volderauer	Vinzenz	13.04.24
MaschMt	Wernicka	Günter	18.10.22
MtrGfr	Zander	Peter	21.03.24

Einzelverlust

MechGfr(A)	Schmelzer	Richard	05.12.24

U-869 crew list

THE HUNTER
The family's first sailboat

In Dry Dock

John B. Moullette

Moullettes at the Helm

Jenny

Dad (the author)

John B. Moullette

Ed e

down to the sea again, again and again

The author stands by to cast off, Stone Beach, Delaware

John B. Moullette

The author, watching the wind, Tortola, BVI

PORTS OF CALL

<u>Outside the United States of America</u>
<u>Countries and Ports</u>

<u>Antilles</u>, Netherlands
- Aruba
- Bonaire
- Curacao

<u>Australia</u>
- Cairns
- Fremantle

<u>Bahamas</u>
- Nassau

<u>Bahrain</u>
<u>Barbados</u>
<u>Belgium</u>
- Antwerp

<u>Brazil</u>
- Fortaleza
- Recife

<u>Cambodia</u>
- Kampong Som
- Phnom Penh

<u>China</u>
- Taku
- Tientsin

<u>Colombia</u>
- Barranquilla

<u>Denmark</u>
- Copenhagen

<u>Djibouti</u>

Egypt
- Port Said
- Suez

Finland
- Helsinki
- Turku

France
- Le Havre

Germany
- Lubeck

Gibraltar

Greece
- Athens

Hong Kong

Ireland (Eire)
- Rosslare

Japan
- Kobe
- Sasebo
- Yokosuka

Korea
- Inchon
- Masan
- Pusan

Malaysia
- Johor Baharu/Singapore

Mexico
- Matamoros

Netherlands
- Rotterdam

New Zealand
- Wellington

<u>Northern Ireland</u>
- Belfast

<u>Panama</u>
- Colon
- Panama City

<u>Saudi Arabia</u>
- Dammam
- Jeddah
- Ras Tanura
- Yanbu

<u>Spain</u>
- Algeciras

<u>Sudan</u>
- Port Sudan

<u>Sweden</u>
- Malmo
- Stockholm

<u>Syria</u>
- Banias

<u>Tahiti</u>

<u>Thailand</u>
- Pattaya

<u>Turkey</u>
- Istanbul
  And a Black Sea port

<u>United Kingdom</u>
- England
  - Harwich
- Scotland
  - Stranraer

<u>Venezuela</u>
- La Guairá
- Las Piedras
- Puerto la Cruz

<u>Vietnam</u>
- Saigon
    - Ho Chi Minh City

<u>Virgin Islands</u>
- Tortola
    - Road Town

Ports of call, continents visited, longitude and latitude lines crossed and routes traversed can be traced by referencing:

Moullette, Ed. D., John B. <u>International Relations, Selected Speeches and Writings</u>.
Tarpon Springs, FL – personal – 1993.
67 pp. illus.

   See:
- Maps of the World
- Countries Visited by Major Locations
- Merchant Marine Discharges (abbreviated)

   Cataloged:
- Library of Congress

YEARNING FOR A SHIP

The author, off Ras Tanura, Saudi Arabia

ANY SHIP

THE MOST RECENT SHIP AS OF SEPTEMBER, 2011

And perhaps the last, but you never know about the "fickle finger of fate."

The *Grace Bailey* out of Camden, Maine. Captain Ray Williamson commanding.
Photo by Fred LeBlanc, © 2002

BIBLIOGRAPHY AND REFERENCE AND/OR SELECTED READINGS

BIBLIOGRAPHY

American Merchant Seaman's Manual, sixth edition. Centreville MD, Cornell Maritime Press, 1994. 614 pp. illus. *

Dictionary of Occupational Titles, fourth edition, volume II. Washington, DC, United States Department of Labor, 1991. 991pp.

Essential World Atlas, third edition. London, George Philip, Ltd., 2001, 177 pp. illus.

Hidden Depths – Atlas of the Ocean. New York, Harper Collins Publishers, 2007. 251 pp. illus.

Ballard, Robert D. with Michael S. Sweeney. Return to Titanic. Washington, DC, National Geographic Society, 2004. 187 pp. illus.

Beilan, Dr. Michael H. Your Offshore Doctor. New York, Dodd, Mead and Company, Inc., 1985. 178 pp. illus.

Butler, John A. Sailing on Friday. Washington, DC. Brassey's, 1997. 277 pp. illus.

Cutler, Deborah W. and Thomas J. Cutler, Dictionary of Naval Terms.
Annapolis, Naval Institute Press, 2005. 244 pp.

Drower, George, Boats, Boffins and Bowlines. Gloucestershire, UK, Sutton Publishing, Ltd, 2005. 231 pp. illus.

Gautreau, Norman G. Sea Room. San Francisco, CA, Mac Adam/Cage Publishing, undated. 311 pp.

Gleichauf, Justin F. Unsung Sailors. Annapolis, MD, Naval Institute Press, 2002. 418 pp. illus.

Hackman, Gene and Daniel Lenihan. <u>Wake of the Perdido Star</u>. New York, New Market Press, 1999. 380 pp.

Herbert, Brian. <u>Forgotten Heroes</u>, The. New York, Tom Doherty Associates, Llc, 2004. 307 pp.

Kurson, Robert and U-869 Partnership. <u>Shadow Divers</u>. New York, Random House, Inc., 2004. 348 pp. illus.

Lambert, Andrew. <u>War at Sea</u> . . . 1650-1850. New York, Harper Collins Publishers, 2005. 229 pp. illus.

Littel, Alan. <u>Courage</u>. New York, St. Martin's Press, 2007. 148 pp. illus.

McCarthy, Tom. <u>Incredible Tales of the Sea</u>. Guilford, CT, The Lyons Press, 2005. 238 pp.

Morison, Samuel Eliot. <u>The Battle of the Atlantic 1939-1943</u>. Edison, NJ, Castle Books, 1947. 422 pp. illus.

Moullette, John B. Ed. D. <u>International Relations</u>, selected speeches and writings. Tarpon Springs, FL, personal publication, copyrighted Library of Congress, 1993. 83 pp. illus.

<u>Noms de Plume</u> . . . copyrighted Library of Congress, 1992. 16 pp. illus.

Offley, Ed. <u>Scorpion Down</u>. New York, Basic Books, 2007. 466 pp. illus.

Prager, Ellen. <u>Chasing Science at Sea</u>. Chicago University of Chicago Press, 2008. 162 pp. illus.

Sandler, Martin W. <u>Resolute</u>. New York, Sterling Publishing Co., Inc., 2006. 299 pp. illus.

Shaffer, Rick. <u>Your Guide to the Sky</u>. Los Angeles, CA, Lowell

House, 1994. 166 pp. illus.

Williamson, Captain Ray. Keeping the Tradition Alive, copyrighted Library of Congress, 2011. 220 pp. Illus.

*The sixth edition of the American Merchant Seaman's Manual – William B. Hayler, Master Mariner, Editor in Chief – is based on the original edition by Felix M. Cornell and Allan C. Hoffman – ©1938.

OTHER

"Das Boot," DVD Wolfgang Petersen, Director, 1997. Amazon.com

Landon, Howard Joseph. Recollections of WWII in the Pacific, 2000. www.georgefamily.net/HJLWWII.html.

Oceanography: Exploring Earth's Final Wilderness. Course # 17301, www.thegreatcourses.com/5econ

OTHER WRITINGS BY JOHN B. MOULLETTE, ED. D.

Selected Leadership Dimensions of Management Personnel in Vocational Education, General Education, Industry and the Military – Doctoral Dissertation, Rutgers University, June 1970

Technical Writing – Masters Degree Project, Rutgers University, July 1964

Training Start-up and Planning Guide, 1989

The Noms de Plume of the Young John Brinkley Moullette . . . , 1992

Collected Poetry of Clarence Earle Moullette – an Anthology, editor 1992

International Relations, selected speeches and writings . . ., 1993

Experiences in Cambodia, July 1993 thru December 1994, July 2007

Platoon 396, 27 June thru 05 September 1944 © 2007, 2013

Danish Emigrants to America, Margaret Dorothy Philipsen, 1900-1967

Significant Dates in the Life and Times of Colonel Charles E. Broyles, Georgia Volunteer Infantry, Confederate States Army, 1861-1906

Experiences at NYC Ground Zero, reported 12 March 2002, Valley Courier, Alamosa, CO, upon request for a written account

ABOUT THE AUTHOR

John B. Moullette, CPL USMC-550622, served two (2) stints in the Marine Corps – one (1) in the western Pacific and China (1944-1946) with Weapons Company, First Battalion, First Marine Regiment, First Marine Division, Fleet Marine Force – Marine Forces China and the second as a Sergeant with Able Company, First Amphibious Tractor Battalion, First Marine Regiment, First Marine Division – Fleet Marine Force – Korea (1950-1952).

John left home at age 16 with a bad case of itchy feet, and wishes he had apologized to his parents for leaving home so early. He also regrets being away so often from his wife, Lillian, and their five children. It was good fortune that she was a wonderful mom and a strong bos'n. John is proud of each of his children.

He lives in southern Colorado's San Luis Valley.

Made in the USA
Charleston, SC
27 April 2016